Original title:
In the Heart of Winter's Chill

Copyright © 2024 Creative Arts Management OÜ
All rights reserved.

Author: Sebastian Whitmore
ISBN HARDBACK: 978-9916-94-608-4
ISBN PAPERBACK: 978-9916-94-609-1

Beneath the Blanket of Snow

Snowflakes fall like feathers,
A cozy blanket on the ground.
The world's a giant snow globe,
Where laughter's the only sound.

Hot cocoa spills on mittens,
It's a winter circus, oh so fine!
Sledding down the wobbly hill,
Who knew cold could feel divine?

Timeless Nature's Slumber

Trees are wrapped in fluffy coats,
Birds are tucked in snugly, too.
Nature's taking a long nap,
While we dance in the frosty dew.

Icicles drip in slow motion,
Like nature's timer, ticking slow.
We waddle in our bulky gear,
Winter style, oh, what a show!

An Overture of Frost

Frosty air and rosy cheeks,
Snowmen with hats made of pie.
Everyone is in good spirits,
Even squirrels whizzing by.

Snowballs flying through the air,
Landing on the neighbor's hat.
Who knew winter could be this fun?
And we're all just getting fat!

The Touch of a Winter's Kiss

The cold nips at our noses,
But we are dressed for the affair.
Giggling as we trip and fall,
Like penguins flying through the air.

Snow, it sparkles underfoot,
A dance floor for our winter glee.
With mittens on our slippery hands,
Each tumble's pure comedy!

Veils of Ice upon Brown Boughs

The trees wear gowns of crystal white,
With branches bent, oh what a sight!
Squirrels dance, they take their bets,
On landslide falls and icy threats.

The ground is slick, a skating rink,
They tumble down, oh how they stink!
With laughter loud, they try again,
Then slip and slide, it's all for fun!

Snow-Laced Reveries

Puffs of snow like whipped cream peaks,
As winter chats and laughter leaks.
Snowmen dressed like fashion stars,
With carrot noses and gumball jars.

A snowball fight, the ultimate test,
With cheeks aglow, we're at our best.
But watch your back, oh friend of mine,
Ambush lies in snow divine!

The Tinge of Sun on a Winter's Dawn

A sunbeam peeks, the chill retreats,
Icicles drip like melting treats.
Birds chirp songs, a jolly cheer,
As frosty scenes start to disappear.

We warm our hands by fireside glow,
And sip hot cocoa as embers flow.
Winter's bite can't last for long,
With melted snow, we hum our song!

Unfurling the Mystery of the Frigid

Behind each flake, a secret lies,
A quirky dance of frozen skies.
Penguins waddle in their sleek attire,
While folks on skis seem less than flyer.

Footprints lead to nowhere grand,
As snowflakes tickle, soft and bland.
What's that sound? A frosty sneeze!
Oh bless you, friend, it's winter's tease!

Haikus in the Snow

Snowflakes tumble down,
Falling like my lunch tray,
Oops! There goes my snack.

Frosty noses peek,
Sledding with a lopsided
Hat on my big head.

Snowman's got style,
Wearing my old scarf and hat,
Fashion? Or a joke?

Icicles drip down,
Like frozen chandelier,
Nature's joke on me.

A Symphony of Shivering Branches

Branches shake and sway,
Whispering secrets low,
Guess they're cold as well!

Squirrels in a rush,
Dressed in their furry coats,
Sipping hot cocoa?

Trees don't mind the chill,
They stand tall in frosty air,
Laughing at our shivers.

Leaves are out of tune,
Making music in the breeze,
Or just losing faith?

The Heartbeat Beneath the Ice

Puddles form in pools,
Wearing a slippery skin,
Dance like no one's there!

Colder than my jokes,
But remember, laughter warms,
Must find my lost glove.

Underneath the ice,
Little fish debate their moves,
Shall we swim or nap?

My toes have gone numb,
Wiggling through the frosty land,
It must be '80s!

Shards of Light on Chilly Mornings

Sunrise peeks so sly,
Bringing sparkle to my yard,
And warmth to my feet.

Breakfast on the porch,
Coffee steaming, wind a-blow,
Oh, watch that mug fly!

Snowflakes catch the sun,
Twinkling like a disco,
Time for the snow dance!

With cheeks frozen red,
I'll still grin like a madcat,
Winter's my new friend!

Frosted Whispers

Snowflakes dance like flailing arms,
As squirrels plot their winter charms.
Hats are worn like goofy crowns,
While snowmen wear the silliest frowns.

Pants of wool, socks mismatched,
All fashion sense has been dispatched.
When snowballs fly, they rarely hit,
Yet laughter echoes, it's a hit!

Echoes of a Frigid Dawn

Icicles hang like foolish beards,
While dogs bark as if no one hears.
A frosty breath that makes us sneeze,
Knitting gloves with stuttering ease.

Sun peeks out, a shivering glare,
Like it's asking if we still care.
Awkward shuffles, a slip, a slide,
As we tumble, winter's wild ride!

Beneath the Icy Veil

The world is wrapped in frosty lace,
With mittens lost, a sock's misplaced.
Hot cocoa spills on frosty floor,
As I shiver, I long for more.

Penguins slide on the icy way,
While I slip like a child at play.
Laughter bounces off the trees,
Forgetting winter's bitter freeze.

Silence Wrapped in Snow

The quiet lands in softest white,
Yet snowball fights ignite the night.
A champ in scarves that twist and twirl,
Grins that shine, hair in a whirl.

Snowflakes kiss with a playful tease,
As we could cackle in the breeze.
With sleds aloft, we're off we go,
Making memories with winter's show.

A Whispering Wind Through Timeless Trees

The trees gossip, snowflakes swirl,
A squirrel's dance makes the winter twirl.
Branches jingle like bells in a tune,
As frost bites the nose of a hapless raccoon.

Snowmen lounge in their carrot-led fame,
Chasing each other, they're never the same.
They slip and they slide, a comical race,
With buttons for eyes, they grin in their place.

The wind chuckles softly, a playful tease,
"Who left the ice cream out?" it seems to wheeze.
Pinecones debate, who's got the best hat,
As snowflakes giggle, "We're cooler than that!"

The Magic of Winter's Palette

A canvas of white, with splashes of cheer,
The snowflakes are artists, no brush to fear.
With a wink of their charm, they paint the cold night,
The colors of laughter, oh what a sight!

Icicles dangle like shimmering smiles,
While penguins in bowties take wintery styles.
"Do I look dapper?" one quips with great flair,
As he slips on the ice, without any care.

Frosty the snowman, with a cheeky old grin,
Jokes with the carrots, "I never wear thin!"
In this chilly circus, joy takes a stand,
As snowflakes perform a soft magic dance band.

A Mosaic of Ice and Time

Footsteps echo, a theatrical show,
As children get caught in a flurry of snow.
They tumble and giggle, in layers they fall,
With hats knitted tight, they've no time at all.

Ice sculptures arguing in their frozen debate,
"One of us looks silly, but isn't it great?"
A penguin throws snowballs with icy delight,
While polar bears chuckle, munching on their bite.

Frost on the windows forms tales of old,
As whispers of warmth, in the cold, unfold.
They chat about summers and sunburns so bright,
With marshmallow dreams on this wintry night.

Footprints in the Frost

Footprints squish in the blanket of white,
With a skip and a hop, they jump with delight.
A dog chases snowflakes, his breath in the air,
With each little pawstep, he's free without care.

The snowflakes debate on who's toughest of all,
As they settle with grace, to blanket the sprawl.
"Who's fluffiest here?" one giggles and flurries,
"Whoever lands last in these frosty worries!"

Sleds zoom like rockets, non-stop through the trees,
While hot cocoa wonders, "Can I join in, please?"
With laughter resounding, they bask in the chill,
In a world sprinkled brightly, with joy and goodwill.

Threads of Silk in the Colder Air

Pine trees wear sweaters, snug and tight,
Snowflakes giggle, a frosty delight.
Squirrels in beanies, gathering nuts,
Dance in the snow, oh, what silly struts!

The sun peeks out, giving a grin,
While ice skaters fall, landing with spin.
Hot cocoa spills, marshmallows fly,
Laughter erupts, as we taste the sky.

Winter's Heartbeat in the Silence

A snowman wearing a carrot nose,
Sings in the breeze, oh how it glows!
Penguins in tuxedos, waddling by,
Tell jokes to the foxes, who giggle and sigh.

Chilly winds whisper, 'Join the fun!'
As children throw snowballs, each hit's a home run.
With each frozen laugh, the world feels bright,
Even the frigid stars twinkle at night.

Glimpse of Life Beneath the Ice

Under the frost, a secret parade,
Fish in their tuxes, serenely displayed.
Bubbles of laughter rise from below,
Making the cold feel like a warm glow.

The bunnies are plotting a snowball fight,
While owls hoot riddle, adding to the light.
Nature's own comedy, written with cheer,
Whispers of joy, echoing near.

The Embrace of Winter's Grip

In the grip of the season, snowmen conspire,
With carrot noses, they dream and aspire.
They build little forts, then laugh 'til they cry,
While ice cubes gossip in cups piled high.

The dogs wear their jackets, strutting with pride,
Chasing their tails as they slip and slide.
Even the icicles dangle and sway,
In this frosty circus, who needs heat anyway?

The Cold Embrace of Dusk

When snowflakes dance like fools,
You'll slip right off your shoes.
The chill nips at your nose,
As hot cocoa quickly flows.

The squirrels wear tiny hats,
While snowmen chat with cats.
They're gossiping, it seems,
About the funny dreams!

In jackets big as ships,
We waddle with our quips.
Yet soon we'll hit the ground,
In laughter, joy abound!

So grab your warmest gloves,
Embrace the snow, my loves.
For winter's chilly jest,
Is truly at its best!

A Tapestry of White and Grey

The world is dressed in fluff,
As penguins play it tough.
They slide and giggle loud,
A bravado, winter proud!

In mittens that don't match,
I trip and miss the catch.
But laughter fills the air,
With every snowball's flair.

The trees wear coats of ice,
And whisper secret spice.
The snowflakes twirl and sway,
In this absurd ballet!

So let's decree a rule,
To dance like silly fools.
For winter's wondrous show,
Is where we steal the glow!

Frosted Whispers of Twilight

When shadows start to creep,
Snowflakes fall like sheep.
I can't seem to find my feet,
As winter holds the beat.

A snowball hits my eye,
From a sly friend nearby.
We're giggling in the cold,
As pranks begin to unfold.

The ice is slick and bright,
We stumble, oh what sight!
With laughter on the rise,
We're the clowns in disguise!

So raise a frosty mug,
To the winter bug!
For in this chill we share,
The fun is everywhere!

Beneath the Silver Veil

With snowflakes in my hair,
I tumble without care.
The world is hushed and still,
But my giggles seem to spill.

The rabbits hop with flair,
While I dance without a care.
Their ears are all a-flop,
I can't help but stop!

Snowmen wearing shades,
Watching all the parades.
They're judging our snowball fight,
In the sparkling twilight!

So let's make lots of mess,
Without a hint of stress.
For winter's funny game,
Is where we stake our claim!

Hushed Secrets Beneath the Cold

Snowflakes tumble, oh what a sight,
They think they dance, but can't hold tight.
A squirrel in mittens, what a surprise,
He slips and tumbles, oh how he cries!

The groundhog peeked from his cozy hole,
Wore a scarf and looked quite droll.
He told a joke to the snowy trees,
They chuckled softly, swaying in the breeze.

The Winter's Serenade

The wind whispers tunes that chill the bone,
Icicles swing like an old windphone.
Penguins don hats to keep their heads warm,
They waddle and slip, what a hilarious swarm!

Frosty the snowman forgot his nose,
Swapped it for carrots and a garden hose.
He sneezes loudly, snowflakes take flight,
His friends all laugh, it's quite the sight!

Frost-Kissed Promises

The frosty air makes noses red,
The cat wears a coat, thinks he's well bred.
He leaps in the snow, then slips with a yowl,
His tail in the air gives a puzzled scowl.

Snowman debates, "Which hat is the best?"
A top hat, a beanie, or one with a crest?
They wear each other, twirling with glee,
Winter's fashion world, a sight to see!

Tales of Frostbitten Echoes

A penguin skates, tries to impress,
Ends up in snow, a comical mess.
With snowballs flying from left and right,
They all giggle in the cold moonlight.

The trees tell stories of winter's charm,
Of critters with scarves all snug and warm.
A raccoon in boots, oh what a scene,
In a world of frost, life's a funny dream!

Crystals of Cold

Frosty flakes in the air, oh what a sight,
They dance and they twirl, a comical flight.
Snowmen with carrot noses that droop,
Look like they've had one too many a scoop.

Icicles hanging, like teeth on display,
They'll drop with a bang, but just not today.
You slip on the ice, do a clumsy ballet,
While your dog laughs aloud, 'What a show, yay!'

Harbingers of Hibernation

Bears tucked away in their cozy little nests,
Dream of honey pots and long summer rests.
While squirrels stash acorns, a nutty delight,
They throw them around, a snowball fight!

The groundhog peeks out, his shadow's a mess,
We're stuck with more winter, I guess, oh distress.
But who needs the sun when we've got hot cocoa?
With marshmallows bobbing, it's a warm, funny show!

Bated Breath of the Solstice

The sun takes its break, quite the lazy bum,
While we wrap up warm, looking rather glum.
There's magic in mittens, in scarves with bright hue,
But I trip on my laces, like once, maybe two.

The solstice arrives, with a frosty big grin,
It sneaks away softly, now where has it been?
Like kids on the playground throwing snowballs galore,
We laugh 'til we cry, who could ask for more?

Frozen Petals

The flowers are frozen, like ice cream for bears,
They shiver and giggle, but who really cares?
A rose with a snowcap looks ready to ski,
While daisies wear blankets as cozy as me.

Petals may freeze, but their colors still shine,
Like a painter's palette, they're saying, 'We're fine!'
So let's build a garden where snowmen can flower,
With laughter and joy, oh, what a great power!

Silent Sighs

The hush of the snow feels heavier still,
But under that blanket, there's laughter and thrill.
Cold noses and paws, a furry brigade,
Creating a ruckus, in snow's grand parade.

Silent? Not really, oh hear that loud cheer,
The world's full of giggles and good winter beer.
So grab your warm socks, let's dance through the night,
With every snout snored, it's pure winter delight!

Harbingers of Spring Beneath Frost

A squirrel wears a tiny hat,
Hopping round like he's in a spat.
Snowflakes dance, all playful and bright,
Even the shrubs are ready for a fight!

The robin tweets with all his might,
'Hey, winter, this is our last night!'
He tries to chirp a cheerful tune,
While slipping on ice, he'll be home by noon!

The snowman's carrot nose is askew,
Telling tales of a summer crew.
He dreams of sunbathing on the lawn,
But for now, he's just chilling 'til dawn!

Under layers, the flowers hold tight,
They're sleeping away this frosty plight.
Soon they'll burst out, colors so bright,
But for now, they just shiver with fright!

A Canvas of Glistening Silence

The ground is painted with sparkling white,
But not a sound, not a single flight.
All the critters tucked in their beds,
Dreaming of sandwiches and warm breads!

A snowflake lands on a puppy's nose,
He sneezes, causing laughter that grows.
His frosty breath puffs up like smoke,
In this winter, even the jokes are soaked!

Chirps from the tree are silenced in snow,
A parade of snowmen begins to grow.
They tell jokes with snowball fights,
Their humor thaws the cold winter nights!

The blankets of frost cover all the land,
While hot cocoa is sipped hand in hand.
Laughter echoes through the chilly air,
As frozen toes wiggle without a care!

Crystalline Dreams in Quiet Veils

Icicles hang like dangling charms,
Waving at passerby with their arms.
Snowflakes whisper secrets in fun,
As they pile up on the old barrel run.

A cat, bundled up, mocks the cold,
In a sweater that's several years old.
Pouncing on snowdrifts, such a delight,
He fancies himself king of the night!

The pond's frozen, a slippery trap,
Ducks slide around with an awkward flap.
They quack in laughter, what a sight!
Performing ballet in the pale moonlight!

The moon grins down, a mischievous sprite,
As children bundle up for a snowball fight.
With warm hearts and cheeks all aglow,
Who knew winter could bring such a show?

The Ritual of a Chilly Night

Gather 'round for the frostbite feast,
Hot chocolate flows, to say the least!
Marshmallows bob like little boats,
While laughter and stories steal the votes.

Outside the wind whips, giving a shout,
But we're cozy inside, there's no doubt.
The cat guards the socks, he's on a roll,
Making sure no one's slipping on coal!

The fireplace crackles with stories old,
Of magical nights when the world was bold.
Card games unfold, with twists and turns,
And laughter ignites like wood that burns!

So let the chill dance outside the door,
Inside is warmth, and so much more.
With friends and cocoa, what could feel better?
Winter nights are a laugh-filled sweater!

The Solstice's Breath

Snowflakes dance like they're on fire,
Sledding penguins, a wild choir.
Hot cocoa spills, oh what a sight,
Chasing snowmen in the pale moonlight.

Mittens mismatched, a fashion faux pas,
Frosty breath, we laugh and guffaw.
Icicles hang like teeth from a grin,
Winter's here, let the fun begin!

Snowball fights declare a fierce war,
Giggles echo as we dive and score.
Neighbors peeking from their warm caves,
Who knew winter could be so brave?

As we trudge home through the night air,
Frostbite bites, but we don't care.
Laughter lingers, it's pure delight,
In snow drifts we crash, a silly sight.

Glimmers in the Frost

Little critters in sweaters so tight,
Making snow angels, what a silly sight.
Pine cones glisten, all covered in ice,
Snowmen plotting a coup—oh, how nice!

Fluffy rabbits in fluffy hats,
Chasing each other, oh look at those sprats.
Sipping hot tea, a steamy affair,
While the world swirls in frosty air.

Jumping in snow, the crunch is the best,
Wintertime giggles, we're truly blessed.
Frosty eyebrows, a fashionable trend,
Who knew cold could be our best friend?

Dancing by fires, our cheeks all aglow,
Hot cocoa spills, we steal the show.
With every flake that falls through the night,
Our hearts grow warmer, it just feels right.

Shadows of the Snowbound

Wandering shadows in the winter's glow,
A troupe of snow people, strutting slow.
Cocoa meltdowns, marshmallows flew,
As snowball battles left a few blue!

Squirrels in scarves, just trying to play,
Chasing the wind, oh where's it today?
Snow-covered branches look like a joke,
With laughter shared among friends, we poke.

Frosty the snowman lost his hat,
He looks quite dapper, imagine that!
Skating on ponds, slipping in glee,
Sliding around like that could be me!

Fireplaces crackling, snacks on the side,
Cuddled up cozy, in warmth we abide.
Jokes 'bout the cold, we all can relate,
Winter's not so bad, just a fun date!

A Chill in the Air

Chattering teeth in a winter parade,
But we've got mittens to help us wade.
Snowflakes fall like glitter from grace,
With frosty cheeks, we welcome the chase.

Worms in winter coats, the squirrels all slide,
While icicles dangle from rooftops wide.
In this snowy chaos, we tumble and roll,
Laughing so hard, we've lost control.

Bundled in layers, we waddle like ducks,
Finding hot chocolate in frozen luck.
With snowballs packed tight, we gleefully aim,
The laughter erupts, it's part of the game.

As the night falls, under stars that twinkle,
Creating memories that make our hearts crinkle.
So let's toast to the chill and the snow's frosty layer,
For winter brings laughter, and oh, such flair!

In the Embrace of a Snowy Slumber

Fluffy flakes dance in the air,
Making snowmen without a care.
But wait! What's that? A falling snooze,
I guess it's time to hit the snooze!

Cats wear coats of white and gray,
Tiptoeing in their own ballet.
The snowball fight is on, oh me!
Where did I leave my cup of tea?

Slushy puddles sneak up quick,
Sidewalks turn to skating ricks.
Mittens lost, it's a tragic tale,
I'd trade hot cocoa for a mail.

Under blankets, we all huddle tight,
Watching movies, despite sunlight.
Laughing at how the cold winds bite,
It's winter's chaos, pure delight!

The Poetry of Frosty Breath

Each breath a cloud, each step a crunch,
Squirrels leap high, oh what a bunch!
My nose turns red, my toes feel numb,
Can someone pass that warm hot rum?

Frosty patterns on windowpanes,
Children giggle, ignore the pains.
The snowman's got a vegetable nose,
I swear he's grinning, goodness knows!

Ice skates on a frozen pond,
Spinning wildly, we're all conned.
Should I glide or take a fall?
Wait, is that my cousin Paul?

The sun peeks out, we cheer and laugh,
Wishing to warm up our chilly half.
But back to pies and woolly socks,
Who knew winter could bring such shocks?

Moments of Stillness Between Thaws

Icicles dangle like pointy spears,
A freeze frame of both laughs and tears.
Kids in boots make a grand parade,
Trying hard not to slip and fade.

The silence sings, the world feels wide,
Where's my skates? Oh, they've gone to hide!
A snowdrift claimed my favorite hat,
Did I leave it near the sleeping cat?

Huddled close with cheeky grins,
Hot chocolate warms our frozen sins.
A marshmallow swimming in my cup,
Winter fun, let's raise it up!

As the thaw calls, we wave goodbye,
To snowflakes falling from the shy.
But winter's charm, we'll not forget,
Until next year, oh don't you fret!

Reflections in a Frost-Covered Mirror

The ground sparkles, oh what a sight,
Reflections play in morning light.
I walk outside, but trip on air,
Snowball fights, beware the bear!

Frosty windows hide a giggle,
Kids inside with a crazy wiggle.
Snowflakes fall like fluffy bows,
While I'm screaming, "Where's my clothes?"

Every doorstep becomes a slide,
Winter madness we try to hide.
Laughter echoes, hear the chime,
As we fumble through silly time.

As spring awaits with gentle grace,
We'll reminisce, oh what a race!
"Remember last year's snowball spree?"
We'll cozy up, just you and me!

Frosty Breath on Quiet Streets

Puffs of breath dance in the air,
Like little ghosts without a care.
With noses red and cheeks aglow,
We march like penguins through the snow.

Fluffy snowballs fly with glee,
Aiming for heads, that's the key!
But ice has other plans in store,
As we slip and laugh upon the floor.

Hot cocoa spills, a chocolate stream,
Marshmallows float, a frothy dream.
We toast to warmth, despite the freeze,
Chattering teeth through winter's tease.

Footprints lead us to the park,
Building snowmen, yes! Let's embark.
Each carrot nose a silly sight,
A frosty friend, what pure delight!

The Parable of the Northern Lights

Up above the darkened sky,
Colors swirl and leap on high.
A dancing show of purple beams,
Like icy sprites in funny dreams.

Why do they twirl? What do they say?
'Come out and play, it's a bright ballet!'
With snowflakes catching in our hair,
We giggle loud, without a care.

'Why so shy, O heavenly glow?'
'We zip and zap, but don't spill the snow!'
As if the stars made a grand bet,
Who can shine without a fret?

So we stare and laugh at the sight,
Sipping tea, bundled up tight.
In frozen hues, we find our fun,
The night's a playground, let's all run!

Melodies of the Snowbird

A snowbird struts, it's quite the show,
Hopping along, with seeds to throw.
Then trips on ice, oh what a laugh,
Wings flapping wildly, doing the math!

With every hop, a song it sings,
Befuddled by all these snowy things.
Its tiny feet make quite the mess,
But winter's chaos brings no stress.

Through snowy trees, it takes a spin,
Pecking away, with a chirpy grin.
'We're cozy here, we'll never freeze!'
It tail-feathers shakes in the winter breeze.

So join the dance, and waddle proud,
With laughter ringing, let's be loud.
'Who needs the sun, when we have fun?'
Says the snowbird, on the run!

Crystal Lullabies in Frozen Fields

The fields lie blanketed in white,
Crystal lullabies whisper goodnight.
As the moon peeks, with a wink so sly,
Snowflakes giggle as they flutter by.

In the hush, frost fairies play,
Twirling about 'til the break of day.
Each twinkle bright with a chilly breeze,
A winter's waltz among the trees.

Hot soup bubbles with a clanking cheer,
While snowmen listen, ear to ear.
'What's that song? Do you hear it too?'
The flakes all shiver, then break into a coo.

With rosy cheeks and hearts so bold,
We wrap in scarves, that never gets old.
As laughs echo in the frosty night,
We march together, oh what a sight!

Ember Glow Amidst the Snow

Snowflakes dance, a wild ballet,
Sipping cocoa, I shout hooray!
Frozen toes beneath the quilt,
A tasty scene, or is it built?

Chattering teeth like little chimes,
Sledding down with silly rhymes.
Hot chocolate spills, quite the show,
Watch the marshmallows float and glow!

Frosty air, a playful bite,
Bundled up, oh what a sight!
Icicles hang, like frozen spears,
Laughter echoes through the years.

Embers flicker, warmth's embrace,
Snowman grins, a juggle face!
Life's a comedy of the cold,
In every laugh, a tale retold.

Echoes of a Frozen Dawn

Morning breaks with frosty breath,
Socks mismatched, oh what a mess!
Brrr-ing alarms with snooze in play,
Lost in blankets, I lounge all day.

Birds don scarves, they chirp and cheer,
Bundled up, they don't disappear!
Snowmen gossip, their noses droop,
Wishing they could thaw and hoop.

Frosted windows, finger art,
Drawing hearts won't warm the heart.
Slipping, sliding down the slope,
Winter fun, it's like a trope!

With every giggle, snowflakes twirl,
In this chaos, the children swirl.
Laughter ringing, pure delight,
Every corner, a frosty fight.

Secrets Wrapped in Ice

Under blankets, secrets hide,
Chilly whispers, snowflakes slide.
Mittens mismatched, but who will care?
Hiding giggles in frosty air.

Sledding's fun till you hit a tree,
"Ouch!" I shout, "That's not for me!"
Hot pies baking, a cozy treat,
Frosty noses, and freezing feet.

Snowball fights, a cunning plot,
A secret stash of snow—why not?
Giggles echo, fun ignites,
As winter dances through the nights.

Luminous stars in coldest skies,
Nature's charm, oh how it flies!
Wrapped in secrets, warm and bright,
Laughter chases away the night.

The Silence of Snowflakes

Snowflakes hush, it's quite the scene,
Whispers float, more like a dream.
Frogs in teacups, why not have fun?
Bouncing off snow, oh what a pun!

Winter's breath makes puppies prance,
Stumbling around in a snowy dance.
Frozen noses, giggles persist,
Frosted lips in a snowy mist.

Slippery paths, we tread with care,
Lost my balance—oh, who will dare?
Every flake tells a story, bold,
Wrapped in laughter, never cold!

Echoes ring as friends convene,
Life's a series of comedy scenes.
With each chuckle, winter gleams,
As joy reigns supreme in our dreams.

Chill of the Wandering Wind

A gust came dancing, oh so spry,
Tugging at my hat and tie.
It twirled my scarf into a knot,
I should have brought a warmer spot!

Snowflakes tickled my nose with glee,
Like wily jesters, wild and free.
They play a game of hide and seek,
Running errands, they are quite sleek.

With every breeze that leaps and sways,
I ponder if it's pillow fight days.
Each flake a poke, a jab, a twist,
Their giggles echo, how could I resist?

So here I stand, in frosty cheer,
Whirling and twirling, drawing near.
With every chill that dares to play,
I'm a winter clown, come what may!

Memories in Ice

A frozen pond, a skating mess,
I slip and slide in winter's dress.
My laughter shrieks, I feel so bold,
Till grace is gone, or so I'm told.

The memory lens of icy glass,
Reflects my failings, one by one alas.
Each tumble down, a tale to tell,
In winter's grip, I cast my spell.

Snowmen grin with noses of coal,
I see my fails in each frigid roll.
Their heads are big, just like my pride,
Who knew this chill could be a ride?

In frozen memories, laughter's warm,
Though winter frosts, I find my charm.
With each chilly fall, I rise anew,
A winter jester, laughing with you!

Starlit Silence Above the Snow

The stars look down, a sparkling show,
"Who's that?" they ask, "In all this snow?"
I wave my arms, but trip instead,
The frozen ground's my tricky bed.

Footprints trailing like a dance,
I prance around, without a chance.
A snowball flies, my aim's quite poor,
Hit a tree, oh what a score!

A quiet night, my laughter rings,
Echoing off the trees and things.
The moon gives chase, with sly delight,
"Come join the fun, you snowy knight!"

In starlit silence, only me,
Making snow angels, full of glee.
With frosty chuckles, I find my flow,
A wanderer lost in winter's glow.

Lament of the Leafless Trees

Oh, naked trees, what have you done?
Bare branches waving, seeking fun.
"Who needs leaves?" they shout in cheer,
"More room for snowflakes, come right here!"

Each twig's a pointer, showing the way,
"Join us, humans, let's play today!"
I climb their trunks, but find a slip,
As winter frosts, I lose my grip.

They moan and creak, a symphony,
Of winter's song, quite merry, you see.
"No leaves, no woes, just playful sighs,
We'll catch the snowflakes, watch them fly!"

With every jolt of winter's tease,
I brace myself, oh, how they please!
Those leafless trees, what a funny crew,
Creating tales, just for me and you!

Shadows Cast by Frosted Moonlight

The moon slipped on its icy shoes,
Dancing over roofs with snowy hues.
A snowman grinned, snowflakes in eyes,
While penguins plotted their heist in disguise.

Squirrels in scarves take flight through the trees,
They giggle at us, 'Come join if you please!'
We slip on ice with the grace of a seal,
As winter's waltz turns our slips into zeal.

The Stillness Wrapped in A Snowy Hug

The world outside is quiet and thick,
With snowmen gossiping, planning their tricks.
Hot cocoa in hand, I laugh at my luck,
Accidentally found my dad in the muck.

Icicles hang like daggers of light,
While frostbite tries giving my nose a fright.
I'd send a postcard, but I can't feel my feet,
Winter's embrace, oh what a chilly treat!

Nature's Blank Page of Peace

A canvas of white, oh how sublime,
But wait! A deer heard me passing by in rhyme.
We both do a dance; it's clumsy in style,
He leaps and spins while I trip with a smile.

Snowballs are tossed, the laughter erupts,
Yet my mittens are soggy, I'm hopelessly stuck.
With frostbitten fingers, I wave through the frost,
Saying sweet goodbyes to warmth that I lost.

Driftwood Dreams and Frozen Streams

The river's a mirror, but where's the fish?
He swam away quick, I just wanted a wish.
With a sled made of dreams, I zoom down the hill,
But ice wrecked my plans; now I'm rolling downhill!

Old logs have stories, I listen and sigh,
As they whisper secrets and flirt with the sky.
With snowflakes as confetti, we dance all night,
In the quiet of winter, everything's alright.

Captured Moments of Frozen Time

Snowflakes dance like silly clowns,
Frosty noses turning red as towns.
People slip and tumble on the ground,
While snowmen chuckle, joy abound.

Sleds zoom by, a wild race unfolds,
Hot cocoa spills, but who cares, we're bold.
Bunnies leap, their fur all askew,
Ignoring the chill, we make quite a view.

Icicles hang like frozen guitars,
As snowball fights wage, we're all rockstars.
The laughter echoes, light and clear,
Winter's a hoot, let's all give a cheer!

So raise your cup, let's toast the snow,
To frosty adventures, we'll let laughter flow.
Captured moments, each giggle sublime,
In this frozen wonder, we'll dance through time.

The Breath of Subzero Dreams

Penguins waddle with a haughty sway,
Curtains of frost, they steal the play.
Dreams of sun, but here we are,
Sipping chill drinks beneath a star.

Frostbitten fingers hold a cup too tight,
As snowflakes tumble, what a sight!
Chattering teeth join the festive song,
In this winter wonder, we all belong.

Polar bears lounge on their frozen beds,
Imagining picnics with cozy spreads.
While frosty breath becomes a cloud,
Winter's parade, oh so proud.

Let's build a fire, roast marshmallows fat,
Witty jokes fly, how about that?
It's chilly out, but that's just fine,
We'll snuggle together, sip warm wine.

Solstice Stillness

Stillness blankets the frosty ground,
While squirrels chatter, lost and found.
Winter's antics, a comic play,
As icicles dangle, glistening gray.

Jackets puffed like marshmallow fluff,
Tripping on ice, it's never enough!
Every step feels like a big show,
With hilarious slips that steal the glow.

The sun peeks shy behind clouds of gray,
Tickling the earth with warmth's ballet.
But sweaters reign in this chilly spree,
We're all just penguins, can't you see?

Giggles bubble amidst the snow,
As we embrace the frosty flow.
In this season of shrieks and delight,
We'll belly-laugh 'til the stars are bright.

Fragments of Frostbitten Memories

Memory flakes fall like glitter bright,
As kids parade in a snowball fight.
Sleds crash, laughter fills the air,
While mom's hot soup is beyond compare.

Snowmen grinning with button eyes,
As we try to build the ultimate prize.
But half the carrot ends up in a bite,
Oh, the joys of this chilly night!

Wrapped up tight, with hats askew,
The adventure brings laughter, ever new.
Snapshots of winter, so much to share,
Each shivering hug shows we care.

So let's make more, both silly and sweet,
In this wintry realm, let's not miss a beat.
We'll gather these moments, our hearts entwined,
In this frosted fun, joy we'll find.

Icicles and Intrigues

Icicles hang, all pointy and mean,
The sneaky squirrels plan a heist unseen.
With every drip, they whisper a plot,
To steal a snack—oh, who'd have thought!

Snowmen gather, plotting their reign,
While kids throw snowballs, causing some pain.
The carrot noses twitch with a scheme,
As they conspire in a frosty dream.

Penguins shuffle, waddle, and dance,
In a chilly contest—give them a chance!
With their tuxedo suits, oh what a sight,
They aim for the ice crown, all through the night!

Thus, winter rumbles, full of delight,
With characters plotting from morning till night.
Enjoy the chaos that it brings,
In this snowy land, oh how the laughter sings!

Embrace of the Winter Night

The moonlight casts a silver sheen,
While snowflakes twirl, a ballerina scene.
A yeti grins from the mountain high,
As snowmen giggle, waving goodbye.

Hot cocoa waits in mugs so bold,
With marshmallow smiles against the cold.
But a squirrel leaps with a daring flair,
To steal those treats—oh, the audacity rare!

Kids bundled up, an army of fun,
Building forts and snowballs until they're done.
A snowball fight breaks out in a flash,
Laughter echoes with every splash!

So dance through the flurries, let good times blend,
With winter antics that never seem to end.
In this playful chill, hearts can ignite,
Creating memories under stars so bright!

Nebula of Snowflakes

Each snowflake falls, a unique little gem,
As children catch them with a joyful hem.
They wonder aloud, 'What shape will they be?'
A glittering storm, oh so silly and free!

The snow drifts pile with a crinkle and crunch,
As dogs dash through, they tumble and munch.
With their floppy ears flapping like kites,
They plunge into snowdrifts in playful delights!

A fashion show struts, all bundled and tight,
With hats too big, what a comical sight!
They twirl in their boots, with scarves that unfurl,
In this wintry wonder, let laughter swirl!

They dance on the ice, twirling with glee,
While parents just watch, rolling their eyes, oh me!
Yet hearts are warm as the cold winds blow,
In the nebula bright, where memories grow!

The Stillness Before the Thaw

The world is hushed, a blanket of white,
Snowflakes settle in whispers of night.
An owl hoots softly, a wise old sage,
While rabbits ponder and turn a new page.

A bear snores loud, tucked tight in his den,
Dreaming of berries and sunshine again.
But winter giggles, no hurry to part,
As frost paints cheeky designs on each heart.

A pair of ice skates just long for the glide,
While children are scheming for slippery rides.
They gather their courage, take off without fear,
And tumble like chubby little deer!

Thus, chaos awaits as the temperatures rise,
Nature stirs softly, opens its eyes.
Embrace the stillness, for thrills lie in store,
With laughter and fun, winter never is a bore!

Frosted Dreams and Fading Light

Snowflakes dance on heads so bare,
Frosty breath fills the chilly air.
Hot cocoa spills, a chocolate mess,
Laughter erupts, who would have guessed?

Sledding down hills, a slippery race,
We tumble and roll, lose all our grace.
A snowman blinks, but it's just our friend,
Who would've thought the snow would descend?

Icicles hang like frozen spears,
Pointing out dangers, fueling our fears.
But we still try to take that brave leap,
And laugh as we slide down, a tummy-deep heap!

In fluffy layers, we waddle around,
Tripping and giggling, plopping on ground.
The frosty air sings, loud and bright,
Let's embrace this chill with all our might!

Serenity in Silver

The world is wrapped in a frosty hug,
Snowflakes swirl like a cozy rug.
But snowmen frown, as they slowly melt,
Their carrot noses, an icy belt!

We build a fort, like kings in dreams,
But a snowball fight's bursting at the seams.
Squeals of delight echo in the cold,
As laughter makes memories we'll hold.

A snow shovel sits, all covered in fluff,
And David builds high, shouting, "That's enough!"
When plow trucks roll, we feel the gloom,
But who can resist a snow-day's bloom?

In the silver glow of our playful plays,
We find joy in the chill, those winter days.
With hearts so bright, we embrace the freeze,
For happiness flows like a gentle breeze!

The Winter's Lament

Oh winter, you come with your frosty charms,
But do you have to freeze all our arms?
Hot chocolate spills, oh what a mess,
Next time, I swear I won't wear this dress!

The squirrels have hidden all their nuts,
While we're stuck grumbling in icy ruts.
We sip on soup and try to stay warm,
Watching snowflakes perform their storm!

Snow boots squeak like a funny tune,
While ice skaters slip, but who needs a boon?
Shovels in hand, as we trudge along,
Trying to find where we all belong!

With scowls and grins, we battle the chill,
Dreams of summer give us a thrill.
Oh winter, dear friend, why must you tease?
For laughter and joy, we'll always appease!

Twilight of the Frozen Woods

As daylight fades, the world turns white,
Creatures darting, a whimsical sight.
Under the stars, a snowball flies,
And laughter ignites, echoing the skies.

The owls hoot with a quirky flair,
While penguins waddle without a care.
Frosty branches wear coats of glass,
And winter pixies shine as they pass!

Chasing our dreams through fields of snow,
We trip on our faces, and up we go!
With mittens lost and noses so red,
We gather round fires, where stories are spread.

Twilight descends, oh what a treat,
As we dance with the chill that tickles our feet.
With cheers and giggles, we bow to the night,
For winter's grimace is a comic delight!

A Web of White Over the World

Snowflakes dancing like they're in a show,
Covering rooftops, making them glow.
Sleds zooming by with giggles and glee,
Hot cocoa spills, oh, what a sight to see!

Snowmen with noses made out of coal,
Wobbly hats that can't take the toll.
Snowball fights where no one can score,
Laughter resounds, who could ask for more?

Icicles glisten, but they're quite a tease,
One sharp drop, and you're done with the freeze.
Winter jackets like marshmallows pound,
Can't find my feet, where's solid ground?

Yet in this chill, we dance with delight,
Embracing the frost, oh what a night!
With cheeks rosy red, we jump and we play,
Who needs the sun on a snowy day?

Through the Window of Stillness

Through glass panes fogged with a warming breath,
I see the kids plotting, avoiding the depth.
In tiny boots, they crunch and they trudge,
Making snow angels, just a quiet grudge.

Cats huddle tight, in blankets they'll hide,
While dogs chase their tails, full of goofy pride.
Puddles freeze under a curtain of white,
Watch your step now, it's a slippery sight!

The squirrel on the branch slips with great flair,
He gives a glare that asserts his despair.
Snowflakes are falling, but oh what a fuss,
Nature's confetti, no need to discuss!

But here in the warmth, with cocoa and cheer,
We sip and we laugh, and forget all the fear.
Cheers to the chill that makes memories bright,
Now tell me, who doesn't love snowy delight?

Glassy Paths beneath Winter's Spell

Sidewalks like mirrors, reflecting the trees,
One wrong step and you're down on your knees!
Skates on the pond, spinning like tops,
Laughter erupts as someone just plops!

Hot tea and mittens, my hands can't get warm,
But outside they're sliding in a snowy swarm.
Penguin-waddles and snowflakes that fall,
"Catch me if you can!"—oh, that's the call.

Down little hills, they dash and they gleam,
Oh what a riot, this whole winter dream!
Joyous shouts echo through frosty air,
Winter brings laughter, who could despair?

Yet inside I ponder, the chips on my plate,
Will I indulge? Or shall I just wait?
In this frosted kingdom, each giggle a treat,
We feast on hot snacks while embracing the heat.

The Art of Winter's Solitude

Snow blankets silence, a hush like a tune,
Sipping my coffee, while birds hum a swoon.
The world seems to pause, not a soul in sight,
Just me and my thoughts in the fading light.

But wait, here appears a ruckus outside,
Ah, those energetic kids take the slide!
Wheels and sleds stacked, a winter parade,
Laughter explodes, my quiet charade.

Snowflakes huge, as if they're in a race,
Grumbling about how they've lost their place.
Fluttering down, they make a grand dance,
And I find myself pulled, caught in the chance.

So here's to the cold, and the fun it brings,
In frosty embraces, even solitude sings.
Life's silly moments tucked under the stars,
Are better with laughter, no matter how far!

Beneath the Blanket of White

Snowflakes dance like they've lost their minds,
Sleds on rooftops, oh what fun it finds!
The snowman grins with a carrot nose,
Wondering where the sunshine goes.

Hot cocoa spills on a woolly sock,
Penguins in parades, who needs a dock?
I'm wearing boots that are two sizes too big,
Slip, slide, and laugh, oh what a gig!

Footprints lead to places unknown,
A snowball fight, and my cover's blown!
Chasing my friends in a flurry of white,
Winter's just silly, what a delight!

Oh, tuck me in, I'm cozy and bright,
Wrapped in layers, a marshmallow sight.
With laughter like snowflakes that tumble and sway,
Let's make winter a game, hooray!

When Spring Waits Indefinitely

The calendar's stuck, oh what a scene,
Spring's playing hide and seek, unseen.
My garden's still frozen, a popsicle patch,
I'm convinced it's a prank, a seasonal catch!

Is that a bud, or a snowdrift's tease?
I sip on soup while the trees sneeze.
Where did the tulips go, what a plight,
I swear they've run off, oh what a fright!

The sun plays peekaboo, with a cloud's sly grin,
And I'm in a parka, where's the warmth you've been?
I bought new flip-flops, just last week,
Yet here I am, in socks that squeak!

I'll twirl with the squirrels in a woolly hat,
Turning my frown into friendship with that!
If spring's waiting forever, let's throw a bash,
In snow boots and shorts, let's make a splash!

The Dance of the Winter Moon

The moon's throwing a party, oh what a sight,
Dressed in shiny frost, glowing so bright.
It winks at the pine trees, all dressed in frost,
"Let's dance!" it whispers, "What a line lost!"

Snowflakes twirl, in a frosty ballet,
While I trip on my boots, oh that's how I play!
Icicles drum on the roof like a band,
I grab my mittens, they're close at hand!

A snowman's a partner, with coal for a smile,
He spins me around — it's a wobbly style.
Twilight giggles, the night's full of cheer,
A symphony of winter sings loud and clear!

When the moon takes a bow and the stars align,
We'll wrap up the dance in a woolly vine.
With giggles and snowflakes as our sweet boon,
Let's give winter a shout-out, the dance of the moon!

Muffled Echoes in the Frost

Whispers of snow, oh listen so close,
The soft crunching sounds as it lightly dosed.
A dog's snowy face, full of mischief and glee,
His paws are all soggy, did I mention that spree?

Hot soup's for dinner, it warms me right through,
I can't find my slippers, I think they blew!
The echoes of laughter bounce off frozen air,
As we pile up the snow in a laughter-filled lair!

The mailman now walks like he's on a tightrope,
While I watch from my window, and can only hope.
That springtime arrives with a wink and a grin,
But winter's just funny, let the giggles begin!

So here's to the frost that makes us all smile,
With memories of warmth stretching over a mile.
Laughter caught in cold, what a perfect blend,
Through muffled echoes, winter's our friend!

A Hearth's Warm Embrace

A hound curled tight by the fire's light,
With dreams of chasing squirrels all night.
The cat plots schemes with a sly little grin,
While visions of tuna dance in her chin.

The cocoa's swirling, marshmallows afloat,
Sipping too much, oh, what a to-do note!
The mugs keep clanking, laughter fills the room,
While dad's socks still rumble, his fashion's a gloom.

Outside the snow makes a soft, fluffy bed,
But the snowman has more style, or so I've said!
A carrot for a nose, and arms made of twigs,
Though he wears dad's old hat, oh, how it digs!

Round the corner, a neighbor slips with a splash,
His dignity gone in a frosty flash!
We giggle and cheer from our windowed perch,
As he vows to conquer, and back he'll lurch!

Frosted Pines and Moonlit Nights

The trees wear coats of powdery white,
While squirrels debate who's best in a fight.
Elves in the garden, they plot and they scheme,
To sneak in our snacks, what a holiday dream!

The moon's stealing glances, a playful old chap,
While snowflakes are dancing like kids on a lap.
Snowballs are thrown with great force and flair,
But the dog brings a snowball right back with a stare!

As night creeps in, the stars twinkle bright,
We build up a snow fort for playful delight.
The neighbors join in with their raucous cheer,
But they'll surely regret it come springtime, I fear!

With laughter and joy, the night doesn't end,
As we gather for cocoa, our favorite blend.
The chill is forgotten, the toast is in line,
As we toast to the frosty, the cozy, divine!

Lullabies of the Icy Breeze

The cold whispers secrets as it teases the night,
While penguins in PJs get ready for flight.
They huddle in circles, with straws for their drinks,
Sharing frosty stories that make all of us wink.

The wind plays a game with the chimes on the wall,
While laughter erupts from the far hallway's call.
Grandma's stories weave magic of old,
While hot apple cider warms hearts with its gold.

Outside, the frost bites, as kids leap about,
Giving frosty kisses, but never a pout.
They build up their castles, each tower a feat,
While claiming the yard as their own winter street.

In the twilight glow, with cheeks rosy and bright,
We cuddle up close, such a magical sight.
As stars wink above, like jokes shared between friends,
We drift off to dreams where the laughter never ends.

Dreaming Beneath a Crystal Sky

Under a canopy of twinkling stars,
We whisper our wishes and compare our cars.
The sleigh bells are jingling, but not from our ride,
It's Aunt Millie's knitting that's far from a guide!

With each frosty flake, we create such delight,
Like snowball catapults that soar into the night.
The neighbors are howling as snow lands with a thud,
While their dog looks bemused, half buried in mud.

The air's filled with giggles and festive good cheer,
While evenings grow longer, with snacks ever near.
Our mittens are soaking from snowball duels fought,
Yet laughter rings out, just like we always sought.

So curled up together, with warmth in our hearts,
We share silly tales and some berry tart parts.
For beneath this sky of crystal and light,
We're heroes of winter, with laughter in sight!

Glimmers of Hibernating Life

Beneath a blanket, snug and tight,
A bear dreams of candy every night.
Squirrels misplacing their own hidden stash,
While mice throw parties, making quite a splash.

The snowman wears the carrot with style,
Winking at the kids, it makes them smile.
With frosty breath they play and shout,
Hiding from snowballs flying about.

In every nook, some laughter brews,
A penguin slide on icy shoes.
Chasing snowflakes, a joyful race,
Winter's not sad, it's a playful space.

So let's embrace the frosty cheer,
With mittens on, let's gather near.
For every shiver brings a fun surprise,
Warmth comes from laughter, laughter never lies.

The Lantern's Flicker in the Storm

A lantern flickers, casting light,
While down the street runs a frosty sprite.
He slips on ice, does a triple spin,
And lands in snow with a goofy grin.

A cat in boots sits by the door,
With paws like snow, she's never a bore.
She plans a heist for the pie on the sill,
Her whiskers twitch as she waits for the thrill.

The winds howl fiercely, a raucous game,
As snowflakes join in, all dance the same.
Together they swirl, a merry parade,
With giggles and squeaks, no plans are delayed.

Beneath the storm's wild, frosty reach,
Silly tales become our speech.
With every gust, a chance to cheer,
Winter's a stage that brings us near.

A Tapestry of Crystal Delights

Oh look at the trees, all sparkling bright,
They tip their branches, what a strange sight.
A choir of snowflakes, they sing with glee,
While rabbits are twirling like they've a degree.

Icicles hang like chandeliers grand,
As penguins waddle, making their stand.
A dance-off begins on the frozen pond,
With every misstep, a friendship is spawned.

Hot cocoa's brewing, let's toast with cheer,
To marshmallows floating, they disappear!
Each cup is a canvas, painted with smiles,
In this wintry world, let's stay for a while.

So gather the laughter, the fun and the frost,
In this tapestry woven, we'll never be lost.
With a sprinkle of joy through the wintery night,
Let's wrap ourselves in these pure delights.

Whispers of Winter's Exhale

Listen closely, can you hear that sound?
It's winter giggling as it spins around.
The frost on windows, a funny tease,
While the dog chases snowflakes, with such ease.

Under the eaves, the ice drips away,
Melting in sunbeams, for some warmth today.
A raccoon sneaks out, eyes wild with mirth,
Claiming the yard is his own little Earth.

Snowman's hat, now askew on his head,
He's caught off guard, not ready for bed.
With a carrot nose that's starting to droop,
He chuckles and sighs, joins the fun loop.

Though chilly winds may swish and sway,
There's laughter hidden in the fray.
So let's wrap up warm and laugh a while,
Finding joy in winter, that's the true style.